And As I Rode Out on the Morning

And As I Rode Out on the Morning

Buck Ramsey

Texas Tech University Press

To Bette and Amanda

This book was set in 11 on 14 Palatino and printed on acid-free paper that meets the guidelines for permanence and durability of the Committee on Production Guidelines for Book Longevity of the Council on Library Resources. ♾

Illustrations by Walt LaRue

Cover design by Kerri Carter

Manufactured in the United States of America

Library of Congress Cataloging-in-Publication Data
Ramsey, Buck.
    And as I rode out on the morning / Buck Ramsey.
      p.   cm.
    ISBN 0-89672-310-0 (pbk.). — ISBN 0-89672-313-5 (book & cassette). — ISBN 0-89672-312-7 (audiocassette)
    1. Cowboys—Poetry. 2. Ranch life—Poetry. I. Title.
PS3568.A4555A82 1993
811'.54—dc20
                                    92-40992
                                        CIP

93 94 95 96 97 98 99 00 01 / 9 8 7 6 5 4 3 2 1

Texas Tech University Press
Lubbock, Texas 79409-1037   USA

Acknowledgments

A few weeks ago, Fred, Billy, Kent, and I gathered up at Marshall Cator's to play and fiddle and sing some of the old songs. Ghosts of Marshall's past saddle pards—of our forbearers—sat around patting booted feet and grinning under their hat brims. Last week, Fred and I pulled up at Dick Shepherd's old wagon where his children were cooking for Hartley County folks gathered at the Houghton Ranch in upper XIT country. We ran into the likes of Roy Mitchell and Bob Morris, and ghosts of their old friends—our tribal fathers—were lolling around soaking up the pleasure. Fred and I were of the generation in between, and we stayed far into the night to join Bob's son, Rooster, and Red to fiddle and sing the old songs for young cowpunchers from the ranches around. I want most of all to acknowledge what those ghosts and cowboys brought to the writing of this poem.

But I took from them, and they never noticed. Lanny Fiel took on the practical task of herding this poem into print. His efforts render these mere acknowledgements anemic. As a candidate for publication, this poem comes from far up a tributary on the mainstream, so even Lanny's boldness on its behalf may have wavered without the encouragement of Susan Miller. Once the poem was accepted for publication, Judith Keeling fought the fights, made the arrangements, tended details. Not enough can be said about the drawings of Walt LaRue, my good friend maintaining a spiritual bastion of the cowboy faith out there in Hollywood. Thanks to my old friends Dan Hawkins and Joe Macrander for their support. And my gratitude to Cindy Scott for encouragement and editorial suggestions. The praise and attention of Charles Gordone and Susan Kouyomjian were more help than they could know. And thanks to family and friends who in one way or another were in on this conspiracy. And what kind of ingrate would I be if I didn't acknowledge my debt to Russia for giving me Pushkin and to Pushkin for the loan of a stanza form?

Foreword

I first heard "Anthem" in 1990 at an evening performance in Elko, Nevada. It was an auspicious introduction to the Cowboy Poetry Gathering. Buck Ramsey's recitation of "Anthem" restored my love of American literature, which had been seriously eroded by the past decade of urban living. (Yet, I had been warned, "One doesn't go to the city to grow fruit; one goes there to sell it.")

Five months later, at the gathering in Lubbock, Texas, I met Buck, after another reading of "Anthem"and talked with him about the possibility of working together on a project for the stage. That September, Hal Cannon asked him to write *Life at the Cowcamp*, which we staged at Elko in January 1991. Again, "Anthem"was central to the performance.

It was not until one Sunday morning in October 1992, however, that I learned that "Anthem"was in fact the prologue to a sixty-four-page poem about Billy Deaver's cowboy initiation into manhood and the unexpected twists and turns of his life that lead to certain understandings as the years pass—understandings that anticipate a new paradigm to replace the old religion of manifest destiny.

That morning, I received a call from Buck inviting me to the final taping of "And As I Rode Out On the Morning." To meet the deadline, Lanny Fiel would rig up a studio of recording equipment, music stand, and reading lamp in the Ramsey living room that Wednesday, and we would begin around 11:00 P.M. after the cicadas, trucks, and nightime activities subsided.

It was evening when I drove into Amarillo from Taos. The winds were blowing hard that night. We arranged ourselves in chairs surrounding Buck, not unlike a campfire setting, and, as night fell, began to record. Soon, very soon, through Buck, we were visited by incarnations of the past—a farmer, a rancher, cowboys, a Texan lawyer, the mother of young Billy Deaver, and, finally, Billy Deaver himself. As the evening wore on; as we worked together; as we took breaks and paced, and taped and retaped; as we allowed a lone truck to pass in the distant night or paused for a cricket's chirping; we managed to clear the way for these old timers to visit us, as they had, in fact, revisited the author at his typewriter. In the doing, we were transported out of that living room to the place of Billy's youth, the cow camps, the site of his trial, and back again, to the conscience of the author, whose epilogue lifted us above the despair, the loss, the lament over the passing of one era with the offer of a beginning for a new one.

Susan Kouyomjian
Bryan, Texas

Prologue

Anthem

And in the morning I was riding
Out through the breaks of that long plain,
And leather creaking in the quieting
Would sound with trot and trot again.
I lived in time with horse hoof falling;
I listened well and heard the calling
The earth, my mother, bade to me,
Though I would still ride wild and free.
And as I flew out on the morning,
Before the bird, before the dawn,
I was the poem, I was the song.
My heart would beat the world a warning —
Those horsemen now rode all with me,
And we were good, and we were free.

We were not told, but ours the knowing
We were the native strangers there
Among the things the land was growing —
To know this gave us more the care
To let the grass keep at its growing
And let the streams keep at their flowing.
We knew the land would not be ours,
That no one has the awful pow'rs
To claim the vast and common nesting,
To own the life that gave him birth,
Much less to rape his mother earth
And ask her for a mother's blessing
And ever live in peace with her,
And, dying, come to rest with her.

Oh, we would ride and we would listen
And hear the message on the wind.
The grass in morning dew would glisten
Until the sun would dry and blend
The grass to ground and air to skying.
We'd know by bird or insect flying
Or by their mood or by their song
If time and moon were right or wrong
For fitting works and rounds to weather.
The critter coats and leaves of trees
Might flash some signal with a breeze —
Or wind and sun on flow'r or feather.
We knew our way from dawn to dawn,
And far beyond, and far beyond.

It was the old ones with me riding
Out through the fog fall of the dawn,
And they would press me to deciding
If we were right or we were wrong.
For time came we were punching cattle
For men who knew not spur nor saddle,
Who came with locusts in their purse
To scatter loose upon the earth.
The savage had not found this prairie
Till some who hired us came this way
To make the grasses pay and pay
For some raw greed no wise or wary
Regard for grass could satisfy.
The old ones wept, and so did I.

Do you remember? We'd come jogging
To town with jingle in our jeans,
And in the wild night we'd be bogging
Up to our hats in last month's dreams.
It seemed the night could barely hold us
With all those spirits to embold' us
While, horses waiting on three legs,
We'd drain the night down to the dregs.
And just before beyond redemption
We'd gather back to what we were.
We'd leave the money left us there
And head our horses for the wagon.
But in the ruckus, in the whirl,
We were the wolves of all the world.

The grass was growing scarce for grazing,
Would soon turn sod or soon turn bare.
The money men set to replacing
The good and true in spirit there.
We could not say, there was no knowing,
How ill the future winds were blowing.
Some cowboys even shunned the ways
Of cowboys in the trail herd days
(But where's the gift not turned for plunder?),
Forgot that we are what we do
And not the stuff we lay claim to.
I dream the spell that we were under;
I throw in with a cowboy band
And go out horseback through the land.

So mornings now I'll go out riding
Through pastures of my solemn plain,
And leather creaking in the quieting
Will sound with trot and trot again.
I'll live in time with horse hoof falling;
I'll listen well and hear the calling
The earth, my mother, bids to me,
Though I will still ride wild and free.
And as I ride out on the morning
Before the bird, before the dawn,
I'll be this poem, I'll be this song.
My heart will beat the world a warning—
Those horsemen will ride all with me,
And we'll be good, and we'll be free.

The Story

WALT LARUE
'92 ©

One

A pattern of the past comes surface
In dapple shadows on the floor.
I stir the leafings there to purchase
A feeling old, one mem'ry more.
Of all the earth, we were its princes,
Though some thought we had flown our senses
When we left homes and sweethearts for
Some place beyond one river more.
The cow trail was the one way going
Directions our kind deigned to take
To places where we chose to make
The mark on time we'd keep for showing.
Oh, we were full of health and hell
And knew the gods had picked us well.

So start with one; his name was Billy.
He'd soon begin his fifteenth year.
His life was common fare until he
Began to hearken out and hear
A far, peculiar kind of calling.
His was a farm boy Michael's falling.
A runty steer had strayed somehow
Where Billy plied the bull-tongue plow
To turn some prairie sod for planting.
His daddy caught him up astride
The plowhorse. He had roped and tied
The stray. (The old dray horse was panting.)
Pa put the horse up in a stall
And laid the law down once for all.

This Billy's dad was grim and gritty—
He'd fit right in Elija's crowd.
If pity showed, he'd himself pity,
Though, all in all, he played it proud.
As railroad arteried a bleeding
From peopled territories needing
A dumping for its detritus,
For all its men whose kind of lust
Caused them to hanker for things virgin,
It hauled them out to bust the sod
That had been sown by some old god
Of prairie passion, grassy urging.
To come, to see, and then conquer—
The civilized investiture.

Young Billy's yens were quite contrary
To frontier nesters like these folk
Whose calling was to break the prairie
To Genesis' Dominion Yoke.
He watched, from where he plowed, the steer herds
Go trailing northward for the railroads,
Edged near the cowboys on their rounds
And liked their manner, treasured sounds—
Those cowboy yells, their jolly prattle,
The lingo spoken, sayings said,
The herd hooves pounding (how they made
The muffled roar), the herd horns' rattle.
Oh, it was something strange and grand
A very few would understand.

The cowboy life was wild and sinful
To nesters like young Billy's dad.
They ran all roughshod and unmindful
Of the old doctrines, acted mad.
He gave his boy a plowline beating,
Just what he thought the boy was needing
For flaunting ways the Old Book God
Had given men who turn the sod.
And Billy plotted out his parting
As afterglow turned into night.
He went away before dawn's light.
But with his shuffling before starting,
His mother stirred from where she slept
And came to him and wept and wept.

She'd been a lass, if you had known her,
You'd surely love when she was young.
But years had worn and beauty flown her.
Now she was torn between her son
And what she still loved in his father.
So now her dread, her deepest bother,
Was that her Billy's years to come
Would be his Pa's years done and gone.
She quietly came. Oh, how it pained her.
She wept and prayed and kissed his face,
For she knew he must leave this place.
Her husband looked for her in anger
To scold her getting breakfast late
And found her bowed by parting's gate.

"This world's a place far too unwieldy
For boys like him to take in stride.
He'll soon be feeling scared or guilty
And three days gone be by your side."
But what she knew he well suspected—
That Billy had been long infected
With callings to the cowboy life
And thought the farmer's way all strife.
A part of him—more so the mother—
Knew that their boy was good and gone
And that to guess where he might roam
Was like predicting next week's weather.
For good or bad, time proved their fears;
He'd not come back to them for years.

Two

And in those years the ancient prairie
Had lived its way for all its time.
The droughts and fires were temporary,
A quirk of weather's fickle mind.
And always, then, it came back stronger.
But now its way of life no longer
Was wholly part of nature's way.
Now money came to make its play.
This prairie now would know "Dominion,"
The bold conceit the Old Book gave
To men of old compelled to rave
The earth was theirs, in their opinion.
(Where was it put: "We are the earth's"?
For surely this was engraved first.)

The railroad spiking north to Denver
Was stretching section at a time.
The railhead now was by a river
Where they would have to halt the line
Until the crew could bridge it over.
With frames of wood and tarp to cover,
A town was raised there by the stream,
A new place where the settlers came
To eat or drink or shop for stocking
Their pantries full of town supplies.
When Billy kissed those tearful eyes,
This was the place of his first stopping.
The boy felt like the dogies feel;
He'd never missed a morning meal.

A boy alone and showing hunger,
Slouched on the boardwalk of a place
Too far from things for boys to wander—
Not boys like this, so good of face—
Would draw a caring man's attention.
A ranchy kind of man made mention
The sun was high enough for chuck.
"I'm peggin' in the best of luck
If you will join me at the table
And talk of things I haven't heard."
Young Billy struggled word on word.
"I'm sorry, Sir, but I'm unable
To pay what they are askin' there.
I need some work to earn my fare."

"Then work you'll get, but I'm not hirin'
A hand too weak to pull his load.
And I don't know a thing so tirin'
As workin' when you've had no food."
Then Billy asked him if he'd reckon
That he could help to load the wagon
The rancher brought to haul supplies.
He felt a slip, a compromise
At taking pay before the labor
The pay was for had all been done.
Young Billy Deaver wasn't one
To take advantage of a favor.
The rancher saw this in the lad,
And this made his old heart feel glad.

"I'll tell you what, my boy, I'm goin'
To eat some chuck they've fixed in there.
The way I see it, you'd be doin'
A fine thing hirin' on right here.
From where old Sol looks from the heaven
He's got the sky divided even.
He's divvied up what's done been done
From all the things that's yet to come.
So don't let Sol catch you alaggin'.
You throw in with my outfit now;
We'll stop in here and have some chow,
And then we'll worry with the wagon.
You say the word, your sal'ry starts—
It's straight up noon, the First of March.

"My name is Oliver, young fellow.
What kind of work you lookin' for?"
His look was good and deep and mellow.
The handshake coaxed him to the door.
For Billy felt the least resistance
To such sincere and sound insistence
Would make him out to seem as one
In opposition to the sun.
"Well, what I'm plannin' on becomin'
Is one cowpuncher genuine.
If you have work along that line,
Then, I can tell you, that is somethin'
That I would gladly hire on for."
They went together through the door.

The bowls had cones of wire for cover
To keep the houseflies from the food.
"I'm glad, my boy, you thought it over
And made your mind up that you should
Throw in with me. As for cowpunchin',
You'll find that my old brand of ranchin'
Will give you plenty chances to
Find out if that's the show for you.
I've plenty land and plenty cattle,
And plenty work to go around.
So if you throw in whole, you're bound
To find that it will test your mettle."
He augured Billy right through chow.
He sort of like the kid, somehow.

Young Billy sensed his life was changing
When he climbed to the buckboard bench
And felt that slow, but sure, first lunging,
The pull away that, inch by inch,
Stretched thin the moorings of his childhood.
He broke adrift, his past prelude,
An island drifting now from him
As he, unfettered, caught a wind
And sailed away into the future.
He was near nausea. Was it fear?
Anticipation? Or the queer
Convulsions of a change of nurture?
No matter now, for this escape
Was buoyed on by the winds of fate.

Three

They trundled over rolling prairie
Of grasses strewn with clumps of brush.
The water of one stream would carry
Them sated to the next. The hush
Of space weighed in but for the birdsong
And buckboard rattle. For just how long
They rode the wagon without talk,
He could not say, but Billy thought
That Oliver seemed very friendly;
He'd point and keep the boy impressed
With prairie things of interest.
Then late when they went 'round a bend, he
Pulled up the team and doffed his hat
And puffed up like an autocrat.

His ranch headquarters in the offing
Lay in the half moon of a stream.
A grove of cottonwood stood lofting
Above the house, the barn, the clean
Lines of corrals, remuda fences.
It was a place for prairie princes.
The house of rock, half in the ground,
Was ringed by bow'rs of vining 'round.
The yard, a patch of watered grasses,
Was sliced by rock-lain border paths.
Down one of these, his better half
Came, followed by a pair of lasses.
Young Billy Deaver thought he'd been
Here somehow, sometime in a dream.

You'd think they'd been apart for ages
The way they held reunion there—
If all their lives were down in pages,
This wasn't one you'd want to tear.
The loving laughter and embraces,
The blending of these fam'ly faces,
Would touch the heart of anyone.
It churned the soul of one young son
Who slowly climbed down from the wagon
And stood back on the other side
Where he could quietly fade and hide
His look, the kinds of clothes he had on.
His mom, his dad, these folks—these girls—
Emotions wafted him in swirls.

Young Billy Deaver's life was changing.
The woman of the house made space
By moving things and rearranging
Her reading room, her private place—
Made space there where the quiet young stranger
Could stay awhile. She claimed the danger
The bunkhouse held for this young stray
Was just too much. She liked the way
He looked, somehow. She felt a longing
She'd felt before—to have a son.
Young Billy was the first among
The bunch of boys for some time coming
Out to this range to make their way
She hoped would settle down and stay.

They decked him down with boots and leggings;
They decked him up with vest and hat;
They geared him out with all the riggings
A cowboy needs to make his tack.
The cantle curved high on his saddle;
The horn was anchored to hold cattle
On his riata of rawhide;
The swells were for the pitching ride.
His bridle of remuda colors—
The gray, the sorrel, chestnut, black—
Were from the fancy braided tack
Of various and sundry fellers
Who'd come to join a cowboy band
And failed to ever make a hand.

The boots and leggings had been Charlie's.
He'd wandered West from Arkansas.
The vest and hat were Jingle Farley's.
He'd gone back home to see his ma,
And, like so many another youngun
Who couldn't hack what had to be done,
Left ev'ry cowboy thing behind,
Discarded all that might remind
Him of his days out on the prairie.
The saddle was Black Jim's; he froze
In one bad winter's blowing snows.
His rope had hung Red Poison Berry.
Some braided reins had once been Ed's;
He thirsted out of broken legs.

They handed him a string of horses
With all the hues of Joseph's coat
And tracing from the blooded sources
Of old Pegasus' faunch and gloat.
And our Bellerophontes mounted
His winged steed and proudly counted
The labors that before him lay,
And measured works to fit each day.
And such were his days in the saddle
The prairie goddess smiled on him
Till sometimes it seemed seraphim
Were riding with him herding cattle.
In fact, such were his grace and skill,
Some jealous god might wish him ill.

Young Billy, mounting in the morning,
Hairpinned the horse in one smooth glide;
Then horse away and boy adorning
Became a centaur all in stride.
He stayed the sunfish and fence rowing,
Stayed all the bronco tricks for throwing
The peelers who climbed on their backs.
They quickly came to him those knacks
Some rode for years without possessing.
Uncanny aimers seemed to guide
His looped riata of rawhide.
And this: he had his pardners' blessing.
Young Billy always seemed to find
The right place horseback the right time.

"I've seen 'em ten hard years ahorseback
Apunchin' cattle for short pay
Not match that boy aboard a good hack,"
The rancher told his wife one day.
"That youngster studies what's around him.
I swear one day out there I found him
Intent upon a cow and calf,
And when I asked, I had to laugh
When he said he was busy learnin'
What momma cows say to their kin.
He hears the message on the wind
And feels the axis at its turnin'.
There are those to the leather born
Whose hearts beat to the hoof and horn."

Four

As Billy tempered to his calling
And took him on the cowboy way,
He naturally went to falling
In bunkhouse compañeros' sway.
His comrades in the saddle ragged him
For living soft, and soon they tagged him
The "Satin Kid" and "China Doll"
For bunking in the boss marm's stall
And taking victuals at her table
And wearing boiled clothes eve'ry day—
Just living in the kind of way
A cowboy only knows from fable.
He grinned and ducked his head away,
But knew he had to change his play.

And in his sleep there came aseeping
A sweetness wild, a shame so good
It sped the pace his heart was beating
And brought about the awful feud
Of innocence with boys at dreaming.
The waking boy blushed at the meaning
The sleeping boy brought to his mind.
He dreamed he topped a ridge to find
A daughter smiling bright and bathing
In clear, clear waters of a pool.
Then he was there, so warm, so cool,
And she was waiting, floating, waiting.
He left his dream upon the sheet
And could not get back to his sleep.

He could not come in for his supper—
He haunted the corrals instead.
Embarrassment came interloper
As through the day he nursed his dread.
She came to him where he was sitting
And took the hand that had been kneading
The blushing flesh all by the brow
And asked if he would please allow
Her one more ev'ning as his mother.
With budding, lovely girls like hers,
The fretful urges, hidden lures
With them and Billy near each other
And sharing time and place alone—
He could not be her household son.

He tarped some sougans for a hot roll
And laced a warbag out of hide,
And cut a scabbard for his pistol,
And belt to strap it by his side.
He rolled his bunk out in a corner.
No joiner, nor was he a loner.
He wisely plied the middle ground
That kept a reputation sound
Where talk was cheap and silence golden
Where private matters were concerned.
He heard his calling, and he earned
The label of a true and bold one.
They told the best of him—just this:
"He'll do to ride the river with."

Those lovely girls, his patron's daughters,
Were even from the length of dreams
And from the length of looks and laughters
A dear distraction making claims
On Billy's sleep and on his musings
The hours he prowled the pastures, loosing
The speculation of his pards,
Who, naturally, became bards
Of bashful buckaroos romancing:
"Oh, by a bower by a spring
Young Billy D. had him a fling . . . "
Their laughter loud, their lingo dancing—
"And when the bossmarm found it out,
His cowpunch days fell in some doubt . . . "

Five

But this fine tale of cowboy romance
Left Billy's whirl in second place:
Poor Dobbin Brown sat all in silence
As Yucca Spear strung out the ways
Old Dobbin choused the widow Horton,
A proper lady he went courtin'
Down out of Denton in those days
They built trail herds for Ira Hayes.
He'd slicked his hair with warm hog taller
And sloshed up good with blossom juice
And asked old Yucca what good ruse
To ply her with that would allow her
To see him with the kind of eyes
That shaped him up about her size.

"Just tell her," Yucca said, "you're earnin'
Your wages horseback punchin' cows.
There's nary woman live not yearnin'
To take in all the law allows
Of us young princes of the prairie—
Though some might tell it quite contrary.
You've got to make her think that you'd
Pulled feats that only top hands could.
Just tell her of your fancy ropin'
When we were skinnin' dead cows out.
Describe in detail all about
You shakin' out your twine and lopin'
To loop that buzzard—how it left
Its mornin' grazin's on your vest."

When Yucca gave him this instruction,
He said old Dobbin swelled with pride,
Commenced to couch the tale in fustian
Detail and prose that would have vied
With Shakespeare Jones, that fine black cookie
Who did Othello for the lucky
Chowhands camped with his wagon band
When Melpomene took his hand.
The widow set her finest table.
From soup to fluffduff, it was more
Than he had ever seen before.
It was far more than she was able
To set before him at one time.
He sloshed it down with her plum wine.

Her table cloth of lace, her China—
Clean white with blue print curlicues—
Old Dobbin never saw it finer
Until it came his time to choose
The bowls from which to ladle helpings.
The cones of silver mesh had kept them
From all attraction for the fare
Till all that hogfat in his hair
Invited houseflies to his dinner.
They made a halo 'round his head.
"It's right fine vittles," Dobbin said.
Such eloquence, he thought, would win her
Esteem and keep her feelings warm
Till he could ply her with his charm.

But here's the tale as told by Yucca:
"So there he sat, his hat of flies
Upon his head as she served supper.
On top of that, the widow was,
You might say, discombobulated—
That does mean, don't it, 'agitated'?—
Concerned about her tableware,
For she quite simply didn't care
For Dobbin's manner with her dishes.
The way he ate, she was afraid
He'd take a bite of plate instead.
I tell you, if her looks and wishes
Could turn into an absent pill,
He'd be long gone with half a meal.

"But hints and looks don't take with Dobbin.
Through eatin', he sinks in a chair
And spurs her rug and goes to jobbin'
A big cigar 'round in the air
Till poor Miz Horton brings a candle.
He settles back and takes a handle
Somewhere along her upper arm,
Then goes to smearin' on the charm.
'T'uz skinnin' dead cows out that summer
And flat out roped a carr'on bird—
A feat you've likely never heard.
Of course, I never figured on her
Upchuckin' on my brand new vest . . . '
That's when he heard her last request."

Now cowboy pards, those friends forever,
They wouldn't let a rift go far
Enough to rend their pact asever.
But all is fair in love and war.
Though Mars could never come intruding,
Sly Cupid might well set them feuding.
But we know Yucca saw the way
To keep this rivals' feud at bay.
He coached his pard on going courting;
He helped him give it his best shot.
And if his luck was not so hot
And Dobbin got cut in the sorting,
We understand how Yucca Spear
Became Miz Horton's "Yucca, dear."

Six

The work of spring was soon behind him—
How quickly they had worked it through—
But if it looked, his past would find him
With little of its residue
Of nester life. *Follow the cowtrail*—
The intrigue, fellowship, travail,
The skill and grace of cowboy life,
If somewhere short of paradise,
Was all he saw when he stood looking
Beside his horse atop a ridge
And asked the gods the privilege
Of seeing where the future took him.
He'd mount his horse and ride him on
Toward the setting of the sun.

For out there they were building trail herds
And pointing them toward the north,
And early on the worthy one girds
Himself to go and find his worth
Among the best ones of his calling
And finds him good or finds him falling
Among the common of the earth.
It might go with a man from birth—
A fate of wonders, or appalling,
A destiny with heaps or dearth
Of joy and love and grace on earth—
Or, willy-nilly, might be all in
The way a man approaches pray'r
Or how he smiles and parts his hair.

"The wife and I will soon be selling
The place to go help make a town.
The foreign syndicates compelling
These landholders from all around
To sell their land and all their cattle
Will leave some folks prepared to settle
And build a town upon a plot
Where there will be a railroad stop.
The missus then can take up teaching,
And I can open up a store.
The missus mentions one thing more:
Our girls have missed out on the preaching
Of gospel we heard in our youth.
Those girls were raised on cowboy couth.

"I saw a picture once of China.
Someday they'll terrace up these slopes
And ship in seed from Carolina
And plant it thick and pin their hopes
On how the seasons and the weather
Bring days of sun and rain together.
Without the grass there'll be no cows,
And cows is all that God allows
The cowboy to give as a reason
He keeps his horses fit to ride.
But for the kind where hearts abide
That pound with hooves, there'll be a season
Of glory yet to fill a life
Before old Time gives it the knife.

"And you're a cowboy, and a true one.
You'll do to ride the river with.
As long as there are still a few on
The range of trails where cowboys wish
Away the plow and stone foundation
You'll ride the horseback celebration
And rock you in the saddle's lap.
A cowboy makes his horse; without
A good horse there can't be a cowboy—
The truth of truths on all the range.
Your heart and mind have made the change;
They'll never make of you a plowboy.
Your horse turns out to be like you;
The way you've turned out, that will do."

But he was saddened as he said it
And turned his head and looked away.
But he continued—he'd prepared it
All through the night. "I've got to say
I'll miss life so much with the prairie.
How can a cowboy ever bury
The urge to be astride a horse
And move to town without remorse?"
Then Oliver was quiet for moments.
"But, Billy, you'll stay with the herds.
A feller can't put into words,
Can't call on those and all his horsesense,
To say what comes into his heart
When time comes for such friends to part."

Seven

And in the morning he was riding
Through low grass hills for that long plain,
And leather creaking in the quieting
Would sound with trot and trot again.
To bless, salute his maturation,
Congratulate the graduation,
Old Oliver had mounted him
Upon the top horse in his string
To ride the Llano Estacado
Until he found a cowboy band
To throw in with and make a hand.
He cut the trail where Coronado
Had ridden in his search for gold—
The first of many, so we're told.

The ocean swells of grass hills rolling,
The second day he rode became
As a calm lake, the breeze consoling
And rippling grasses on the plain.
His vision, loosed to each direction,
Filled Billy with exhilaration
A hawk must know on its first flight
When all the world seems in his sight.
He watched his image in that mirror
That hangs on some wall of our mind,
And there he rode; he rode so fine,
So aching proud as he rode nearer
This place of testing, trial more
Than he had ever known before.

But first he suppered on a sundown
That he'd remember as he died.
A bank of crimson clouds there shined on
The playa lake he camped beside.
In morning he veered north in break lands
Where some outfit had spread its cowhands
To gather out its creeks and draws
To build a herd—at least it was,
He hoped, the range for which directions
Were drawn for him upon the ground
When Oliver had sent him bound
For this place where the old protections
Of friends and kindred now were gone
And where he was all on his own.

He rode the long rim of a mesa
And reined up at its farthest peak,
And, lo, he looked upon a vista
Would fill a thousand dreams. How quick
The blood rushed through his heart. No vision
Could ever more reward decision
A kid made picking out a path
As time was coming at him fast
Than when upon that promontory
He saw those cowboys hold a herd
That smoothly churned and slightly stirred
The dust of leagues and leagues of prairie.
The dreams this vision long would fill
Were not all his. I dream it still.

He stayed and drank until the gloaming
Of prairie dust and yell'wing light
Brought to his cowboy breast a longing
To low'r himself into the sight.
The hands were rounding in to supper.
The cookie and his hoodlum hustler
Prepared the fixings at the fire
To feed the punchers gathered there.
As Billy rode up to the wagon
One waddie, quite the worse for wear,
Poked up a greeting in the air.
"Well, light and hitch a grub bag on.
You look to be a boy in need
Of some of Coozinary's feed."

Young Billy asked the friendly waddie
If he could speak to their boss man,
And he was pointed to a jaunty
And jolly bunch that seemed less than
Full occupied with trail hand duties.
In fact, they laughed at ribald beauties
A man of diff'rence told to them.
The cowboys all seemed drawn to him.
He wore a diff'rent cut of clothing;
His boots, though dusty, were unscuffed,
His pant legs in high boot tops stuffed.
His hat crease, spurs, bandanna—nothing
Would fit him in this cowboy band—
He seemed, well, something fine and grand.

Another from among those gathered
Came ambling out toward the kid
When the old cowboy who had favored
The kid with welcome called to bid
Them notice that they had a caller.
This one, he, too, seemed to walk taller
Among the cowboys of the crowd,
As if he was the one allowed
To call the shots, to act as leader,
The wagon boss of that trail drive.
He flashed a grin, and a moonrise
Shone in the dust bank of his feature.
"You'd better light and perch awhile.
No other chance for many mile."

Young Billy felt at ease and welcome.
Though shy, he was a straight out lad.
And, standing there, he looked to be some
Dear mother's son who might be glad
To rest a spell and whack some vittles.
"Though when you hear how Coozy fiddles,
Your ears might sour the stomach's work."
Young Billy toed around some dirt
And said, "I rode off out here lookin'
To throw in with a cowboy band
And show 'em I can make a hand.
And I could surely stand some cookin'."
They one and all gave him a smile,
As if he'd do to keep a while.

When he had horse and saddle tended,
They formed a grub line at the pots.
The foreman sort of recommended
The two lone riders draw for lots
"To see who'd be the first for takin'
Of Coozinary's Dutchpan makin'."
The noble one took Billy's arm—
His look, his touch was friendly, warm—
"I'll cast my vote for this young stranger."
You looked at him as look you may,
But when he looked you looked away.
He might be godsend, might be danger—
But it was clear he was the kind
Who loomed and lingered in the mind.

The short time he'd been life's sojourner
This kid had never known the thrill
Of being singled out for honor.
On top of that, and better still,
The man conferring it, in stature,
Was blessed the best by Mother Nature
Of all the men he'd ever seen.
Had this whole hour been but a dream?
The cowboys voted with the tall one.
Young Billy headed up the line
Of chowhounds hankering to dine.
He wondered, eating, what you'd call one—
A boy, like him, out wand'ring, lost,
Who happened on this kind of host.

When Billy sat and started eating,
The others pulled a ways apart.
They gathered like a group in meeting,
And laughed like cowboys on a lark.
And once when he looked their direction,
He looked away in stark reaction
To fulsome looks that came his way.
Against his mood, he felt like prey
A fleeting moment. But their laughter
Was comforting—men having fun.
He settled back to soak some sun.
Whoever had a benefactor
To match this wagon crew of men?
He closed his eyes and gave a grin.

Then something in the air turned chilly,
As if a cloud passed by the sun.
"We need to ask some questions, Billy,
Concerning what you might have done
As you came riding to these break lands,"
The foreman said. The other cowhands
Stood hov'ring back like birds of prey
To be assured the victim lay
Defenseless there. The wagon foreman
Gave him a grin, half-turned and made
(In short, young Billy was afraid)
A motion like a Stygian doorman.
The hour that was the best he'd known
Was suddenly, now, done and gone.

"There's something more than this appearance
Of some young button wantin' work.
We know that nosy interference
Into what in the mind might lurk
Is crossin' o'er the line that's proper
Amongst this tribe of rider-roper.
We voted, though. It seems the score
Is for you tellin' us some more.
We'll see you have an even hearin'.
We're not the kind to try a case
And not consider all the ways
A feller claims the truth can clear him.
He'll prosecute—him in the duds.
I reckon I will be the judge."

Eight

Five good and true men were selected
To be the jury in the trial,
Because with five, it was suggested,
They couldn't vote a tie. Meanwhile,
The wagon cook, a fiddle player,
Had knelt down with the kid in prayer
To tell the bosses up above—
He prayed to Yaveh, Zeus, and Jove
And gods that numbered in the dozens—
"The kid might well be on his way
No matter what I have to say,
So tell his uncles, aunts and cousins,
His grandfolk—kin who've gone before—
To make a place for one kin more."

"Since you seem his chief sympathizer,
Well, Coozy, you can take his case.
You're not known as a compromiser
In any cause that you embrace."
The trail boss seemed again right friendly.
"I reckon he's as good as any,"
He said, and gave the kid a smile—
The last he'd get for quite a while.
A sougan-covered water barrel
Was this proceeding's witness chair.
The kid, the only witness there,
Was told, "Take off that top apparel—
The kerchief, take the collar loose
To measure for the hangman's noose."

"Well, settle down, this court's in order.
This button here is now on trial.
And even though us cowboys sorter
Admire his looks and like his style,
There's bound to be a law he's broken.
So there it is. The judge hath spoken."
He pointed to the suited man,
Who paced a moment, then began
His lawyerly examination.
"I'll ask, you answer straight and true
Is the advice I'd give to you—
And all in your dire situation."
His deep voice stroked the empty air
And Billy tried to think a prayer.

"Your name?" "My name is Billy Deaver."
"Your loved ones, where do they abide?"
"The railroad stops there at the river.
My daddy's farm's the other side
Of where that little town's asettin'."
"You mean you left your folks afrettin'
And roamed these many miles? Explain."
"My daddy whipped me with a rein
For ridin' Ball and ropin' chickens."
The cowboys laughed. "One whipping, you
Thought leaving was the thing to do?
A growing boy must take his lickings.
And what did your dear mother say?"
"She cried and said don't go away."

"You left your mother—broken, weeping?
You turned your back and went away?"
"I tried to tell her I was keeping
A promise I made as I lay
One night all marked up by the plowline
My pa had whipped me with. At that time
I told myself I'd go away
Before the breakin' of next day
If Pa gave me another beating.
I swore I'd join a cowboy band
And ride out here and make a hand.
It broke my heart, my mother pleading,
As she fell crying to the floor
For me to be her boy some more."

Some dirty cheeks were getting muddy.
Those cowboys all had left a home,
Had heard a plea—"Oh, please, my buddy,
Don't leave me to forever roam
Out on that wide and lonesome prairie.
Climb from your horse and with me tarry.
For out West where the bullets fly,
Could be you'll lay you down and die
And we'd not know where you had fallen
Or how or when you met your end . . .."
So they were getting out of hand.
They liked this kid. So he, the tall one,
Knew he must coax them in his sway
Before the kid stole them away.

"Tell us, as you on your way wandered
For pleasure as your mother wept,
As you so nonchalantly sundered
The string with which your mother kept
Her little fam'ly tied together—
We wonder, could you tell us whether
The trail you took to here was straight
And narrow? Or, lad, did you mate
With mischief as you came west riding?
There's many day has passed between
The day you pulled that parting scene
And now. I ask you, are you hiding
Some darker deeds you might recall
If truth would have you tell us all?"

"No, there was nothing on my way here
I did that you could say was bad
Enough for this . . . but . . . let me say here . . ."
(Young Billy blushed, because there had
Rushed to his mind those private matters
When he had dreams of those fair daughters
Of Oliver. He turned his face.)
"We struck a chord, I see. So, yes,
Just tell us now what you were thinking
That caused the blush, the hidden look."
But Billy cleared his mind and shook
His head. Such dreams, they could not link him
With deeds deserving this abuse—
Much less the swinging hangman's noose.

No trees around, they'd used the wagon
By hoisting up its lengthy tongue,
Then ran the rope where it was sagging
There still and full-noosed. "All right, Son,
I think it's time that you were telling
The rest of it. What kind of helling
Were you up to in all this time
From when you left your home behind
To when you rode in here, all smiling,
To these boys' hospitality.
The thing I'm getting at, you see—
We'll set aside all that beguiling
Young cowboy's act of leaving home
To be forever on the roam—

"We know the brand your horse is wearing,
And where he got his daily hay.
There's nowhere near folks so endearing—
Pike Oliver and his wife, May —"
At mention of his friends, the witness
Began to regain some old fitness—
Relief came clearly to his face.
"They took me in. And at their place
I learned the cowboy way of doing.
He told me I was good enough
That if I came and showed my stuff,
There was no doubt that I'd be going
Up that long trail right by your side.
There's nothing there I need to hide."

This kid was fairly well disarming
The prosecutor's charge at him.
"A long riata means, 'Take warning:
This roper finds your brand too dim
To certify you are the owner
And figures you should be a donor
To his new growing cinch-ring herd.'
I ask how many brands you blurred
And burned back in more to your liking?"
"I only shook my rawhide loose
To snare some bear grass in its noose,
Or stakes where surveyors are spiking
Their measure of the old Staked Plains."
He clearly wasn't making gains

Against the innocence exuding
From this straightforward, mannered boy;
No need continuing alluding
To implied misdeeds with this ploy.
The prosecutor mulled while kneading
A manly chin. He knew his pleading
Must take a very different course.
"I need not waste my time and yours;
There's plenty evidence already,
My friends, your honor, jurors true,
To judge the boy, give him his due.
Let's keep our justice sure and speedy.
My final plea must wait its place.
Your honor, friends, I rest my case."

Nine

He takes his hat and combs his fingers
Back through his wavy raven hair.
He grandly sits, his great voice lingers
A moment on the hushing air.
"All right— " the boss, the judge injected,
"This young man's rights must be respected.
So Coozy, you now have the floor
To try and even up the score.
As it stands now, I'd say your client's
A dough pan full of points behind.
I know your tricks, so keep in mind
The court expects your full compliance
With its new rule: It's coming dark;
You've got one minute for your part."

"Did you not tell us boys, young loner,
You rode out here to show your stuff?"
"Yessir." "I rest my case, your honor.
For me, that's plenty good enough."
"Good. No more evidence imposing,
You do your arguments in closing.
Now, Coozy, since you have the floor,
I'll let you go a minute more
To tell us how this boy's not guilty."
So Coozy up and sang away
Like some buffoon in some stage play:
"Oh, lolly, lolly, lolly lilty,
Oh, he'll not see his mother when
The work's all done this fall. Amen."

"Let's let 'im go," a cowboy hollered
From out there in the gallery.
"Well, Coozie's plea must now be followed
By Temple, what he has to say.
This jury can't make a decision
Until this court fulfills its mission
And gives each side an equal time.
To make a case of this boy's crime,
It's Temple's turn. The judge hath spoken."
Then even prairie sounds of dusk
Fell silent— nor did even gust
Disturb the hush that went unbroken,
As if the gods held all at bay,
Awaiting what this man would say.

He rose and stroked at one lapel
And with his left hand took his hat,
And ev'ry cowboy there could tell
This wouldn't be a reg'lar chat.
There was such power in his manner,
It would have been that moment saner
To take on Plato in his den
In front of Athens' brightest men
Than stand in open opposition
To this man grandly standing there.
He swooped his hat across the air
In humble, artful recognition
That all those cowboys there would each
Pass judgment on his closing speech.

And in those moments of his sounding
His voice filled all the empty air
And all the minds of those around him,
Struck all those nerves that were laid bare.
And even Billy Deaver, bless him,
This sounding voice did so impress him,
His wonder took away his fear
Though prospects for his doom seemed clear.
"Your honor, all my lonely brothers,
I know the places of your heart
Grown soft that day you each did part
With sweethearts, folks, your dear, sweet mothers,
How tears as you your watches keep
Fall drop by drop, and on your sleep.

"And ride you do now, wild and free, boys.
Duality, though, plies its course,
And, quietly now, you look and see, boys,
How your high yelping can grow hoarse
That celebrates this life you're leading.
As memory doth make its pleading,
You take the measure of its joy
By fading echoes. Yes, cowboy,
For you have left your mother weeping.
Now you eat dust and you nurse pain;
You shudder, sweat, and where's the gain?
And what gods are your vigil keeping?
And do they smile or do they rave
As you ride near your lonely grave?

"Let us approach, entreat sweet Reason
To smile on you and bring relief
To you this long and lonely season
Ahorseback out here, bring surcease
From mem'ry of your mother weeping.
I offer you, my friends, in keeping
With long tradition, now a chance
To expiate your circumstance.
Recall old Abraham and Isaac—
How common has been sacrifice,
The offering of precious life
That makes our conscience, like the lilac
That blossoms bright and fresh anew,
Grow clean when all is paid its due.

"Your high esteem for this young stranger
Who comes to follow in your trail,
All absence of revenge and anger
If you should vote him from this vale
Of mortal toil—how could a better
Or simpler chance to please and cater
To all those forces that control
Our fate and fortune, game and goal,
Present itself. For you to offer
This good young lad in sacrifice
Would be a gesture just and wise
And certainly would make much softer
The pillow of your prairie sleep
And let your heart its comfort keep.

"Recall, my friends, young Isaac never
Did break his mother, Sarah's, heart.
If your love for this boy could ever
Match Abraham's, I miss my mark.
You get my point. The sacrificing
Of this good lad—while not enticing—
For expiation of the guilt
Of all at once, all you who left
A mother, sweetheart, broken, weeping,
It's, well, a simple thing to do
For the advantage it brings you.
Yes, hang he must, I say, in keeping
With punishment for his sad part
In breaking his poor mother's heart."

Ten

Among the cowboys a contagion
Of muddy tears had spread throughout.
Then first a "bravo" by the wagon,
And then they all began to shout,
"Yes, bravo, yes, hooray the hangin',"
As each began a hearty banging
Upon another cowboy's back.
"Quiet down, there's still another act—
Or two, if there's to be a walking
Upon the air by this good lad.
It's time the jury made its sad
Decision. And I'll have no balking.
It's good those cattle are at home
Or they'd stampede and be long gone."

The wagon boss, the judge, was trying
To calm the crowd and get things done.
But with the yelping, laughing, crying,
Those cowboys sure were having fun.
"If you boys make our cattle scatter,
This whole damn show won't make no matter,"
The wagon boss called to his boys.
"Let's tie a muffler on this noise,
And, jury, let's hear your decision.
Now, come on, boys, let's gather 'round."
So things began to settle down
As each took back his old position
And waited for the jury to
Pronounce the fate the kid was due.

They didn't wait too long; the jury
Announced its verdict right away.
"They vote he hangs. But there's no hurry
If Coozy has some more to say
On his behalf. The judge hath spoken."
So Coozy rose, then made a token
Appeal—in fact, he merely shrugged,
And then walked over there and hugged
The kid and made a futile gesture.
"I reckon that's all I can do.
I leave the boy's fate up to you."
"If he's to hang, I guess a lecture
Would do no good. So, here's the deal:
He'll wrestle Stump for his appeal.

"And if he wins, there'll be no hanging."
Now, Stump was Coozy's hoodlum help,
A sturdy dwarf, who, fully standing,
Would match his height if Billy knelt.
The cowboys whooped again at hearing
There was a chance at persevering
In his young life yet for the kid.
(In truth, they cheered because the lid
Was not shut on their entertainment.)
But what they felt was nowhere near
The surge of sudden, blessed cheer
That came upon our young defendant.
He saw the dwarf, smiled at the noose,
And figured he'd be soon turned loose.

But many trying minutes later,
The cheer he'd felt had all been drained
Upon the mat of grass. A crater
Now gapped where confidence had reigned.
Despair in his young soul was creeping
Like stinging sweat that now was seeping
In hide rubbed raw by brittle grass.
That dwarf named Stump, locked hard and fast
Across his breast, had proved as sturdy
As some tree trunk, a stubborn ant
Pushing a load he knows he can't
Go home without. His mind now murky,
Young Billy's will was nearly gone.
Then—one heave more and he was done.

That one last thrust for his survival
Brought cheers from all the audience.
They hoped for just one more revival
That would have added some moments
To this great show. But all their cheering
Came faintly to young Billy's hearing
Like echoes of a distant yell
From down a canyon or a well.
He'd nothing left to give the tussle.
The dwarf rolled off and let him lie
To rest a while so he could die.
And Billy didn't move a muscle.
He was so spent he merely sighed.
He didn't care much if he died.

The suited man came, knelt beside him,
And eased his head up from the ground.
"This fine young lad, I think I like him.
I'd say his character is sound.
There aren't three cowboys with this wagon
Who could have wrestled that dwarf dragon
For quite as long as this young man.
There's no doubt he'll make you a hand.
So, son, you've been initiated
Into the true cowpuncher tribe.
So, long and happy may you ride.
Now, it would be appreciated
If you'd see to this cowboy's need,
And have someone bring me my steed.

"I've miles to ride if I'd be keeping
Appointments I am sworn to keep."
And suddenly he fell to weeping,
And Billy in his arms did weep.
But in a moment he was mounted
And rode away from the anointed
Young cowboy, sobbing in the grass
And wond'ring what had come to pass.
Well, Coozy and the trail boss washed him
With cool wet cloth. One softly spoke,
"Well, Coozy, seems our little joke,
The way it came off, might have cost him
A bit of youth, delayed his plan.
But we have ourselves quite a man."

Those cowboys' lives were sometimes boring.
When Temple Houston came around
Some heady hours could take to soaring
On all those words eight to the pound.
They'd take a break and grab some pleasure
In days that daylight failed to measure.
Young Temple was Sam Houston's boy—
He was the Raven's pride and joy.
Old Sam, Young Temple, Little Billy—
Down there in Texas myth emerged,
Some lines to create, when converged,
A lineage that, willy-nilly,
Might crown the Moon and glove the Sun
As it draws nigh Millennium.

Epilogue

WALT LARUE
92 ©

A Ponder

And was I real or was I dreaming?
Was I that boy, "so good of face"?
Were we so good, or are we scheming
To forge a role that garners grace?
We rode our horses 'cross the grasses
In flight from Babel's huddled masses.
We were the offside of the coin;
We didn't care to court or join
The mad pursuit of pelf or puissance;
We left our money on the bar—
A crude disdain, perhaps, but far
Contrary to the crass insistence
On hierarchy's servility
That passes for civility.

We didn't spend much time defining
Our role, but were we to define:
"To do what's right with careful timing,
To be the right place the right time,"
Would pretty well sum up our duties.
We learned by look and feel, not studies—
Unless it was the moves of pards
Ahorseback, eloquent as bards.
It was a spark, and we would fan it
While riding favored by good winds
With favored ancients, proper ends.
The owners merely mined the granite;
We were the sculptors of the herd.
Yes, ours the poetry; theirs the word.

The Goddess handed me the bridle
That tamed my horse's summer heart.
Then, by the spring and standing idle,
He took my saddle, took his part
In works of rounds I would be keeping.
In consecrating moonlight meeting
I joined myself to Mother Earth
And put in order first things first.
I pledged my heart; I made my promise
To love her faithfully till death
Despite enigmas, even with
The burdens of those moods that harm us.
I joined to her in mortal cord
To tender thought and work and word.

We toil so hard in sun, we're abler
By light of moon to know our part.
So things that I would take from labor
I'd carry only in my heart.
The death millenniums behind me,
Lift up the stone and you will find me.
The true man dwelling in the dream,
I listen and remember when
Each thing was sung into existence
And carried yet its proper name.
The Moon might bring that time again
If it can calm the Sun's resistance.
Beyond the din of dusty day
There is no closed place I must stay.

When thought is clear, things fall in place,
We'll grasp the mood of Nature's face,
We'll know the texture of real grace.